Talking to Your Children about Race

A Biblical Framework for Honest Conversations

Jerome Gay Jr.

New Growth Press

newgrowthpress.com

New Growth Press, Greensboro, NC 27401
Copyright © 2022 by Jerome Gay Jr.

Unless otherwise indicated, Scripture quotations are taken from
the Holman Christian Standard Bible (HCSB). Copyright ©
1999, 2000, 2002, 2003, 2009 by Holman Bible Publishers,
Nashville, Tennessee. All rights reserved.
    Scripture quotations marked ESV are taken from The Holy
Bible, English Standard Version. ESV® Text Edition: 2016.
Copyright © 2001 by Crossway Bibles, a publishing ministry of
Good News Publishers.

Cover Design: Dan Stelzer
Interior Design and Typesetting: Gretchen Logterman

ISBN: 978-1-64507-267-6 (Print)
ISBN: 978-1-64507-268-3 (eBook)

Library of Congress Cataloging-in-Publication Data on file

Printed in India

29 28 27 26 25 24 23 22   1 2 3 4 5

Conversations about race and ethnicity can be uncomfortable. Often parents don't know what to say or how to say it. It might seem easier to duck a hard, confusing subject, but your children are learning about race already. They are being taught by the news, social media, educators, their peer group, and even from your actions and attitudes how to view differences between people groups. But are they hearing what God has to say in the Bible? Having conversations about race will give you an active role in ensuring that your children are given a biblically rooted and gospel-saturated view of race and ethnicity.

It's vital that you don't miss this opportunity to give your children a biblical framework to tackle this topic. Along the way you will also be giving them a blueprint for how to approach any difficult subject.

Start with a Biblical Framework about Christian Unity

Before we talk about strategies and steps, it's important to have a biblical framework for how to approach the topic of race.

First, Scripture presents us with a beautiful mosaic of humanity created by our Triune God. The truth is that when it comes to race, while we all may not share the same color, our varying colors are an expression of God's creative genius (Psalm 139:14). The apostle Paul, when sharing the gospel in Athens, points out that, "From one man [God] has made every nationality to live over the whole earth and has determined their appointed times and the boundaries of where they live" (Acts 17:26). While our colors differ, we all share the same ancestry. And, in Jesus Christ, the gospel is for every tribe, nation, and ethnicity. It's faith in Christ that brings us into God's family—not our ethnic background (Ephesians 2:8–9).

Second, the Bible makes it clear that God opposes racial or ethnic prejudice. This can be seen in how Paul confronted Peter when he came to visit the Galatians. Peter acted one way around Jewish people and another way around Gentile (non-Jewish) people by distancing himself from fellow Christians when his Jewish friends showed up. Peter's behavior was so detrimental and unbecoming of someone who claimed faith in Christ that Paul had to oppose him to his face in front of others. Paul didn't go behind Peter's back, nor did he ask anyone else what they thought about Peter's behavior; he approached him directly and firmly. How amazing that a Jewish man confronted another Jewish man on his partiality and prejudice (Galatians 2:11–21)! What made him do that?

- Paul spoke so strongly because the gospel of Jesus Christ was at stake. Peter was the apostle who received the vision of all who had faith in Christ being welcomed into God's family (see Acts 10), regardless of ethnic background. But in Galatia, Peter acted as if following Jewish customs were necessary to be included as full members of God's family. His actions said that faith in Jesus's sacrifice was not enough—more had to be done. Paul spoke out against Peter to defend the gospel.

- Paul spoke so strongly because the church in Antioch was ethnically diverse. Antioch was where we heard the term "Christian" used for the first time (Acts 11:26). Paul did not want them to think that their righteousness could be gained by observing the Jewish law (Galatians 2:21).

- Paul spoke so strongly because the missionaries who were sent from Antioch were diverse: Barnabas—Jew of the diaspora; Simeon called Niger—most likely African; Lucius of Cyrene—a Cyrenian Jew, like John Mark who wrote Mark; Manaen, friend of Herod the tetrarch and Paul—Jewish (Acts 13:1–3). It was important for them to know that following Jesus was not based on their ethnicity but on their faith.

What would make Paul go from standing with Peter in Jerusalem (Galatians 1:18) to standing against him in Antioch? Paul was standing against duplicity in behavior and deviation from the gospel. If the authenticity of the gospel is to be upheld and unity is to be achieved, you and I can't shy away from speaking out when we see the unity of the body of Christ threatened. And we can't shy away from sharing these life-changing truths with our children. The heart of the gospel is that we are all saved by faith, not by our religious law-keeping or our ethnic background. In Christ we are all one, and that is a truth worth defending!

A Biblical Perspective on Racism as Sin

There are many definitions of racism that people use for different reasons. But as we noted, racism is rooted in the sin of partiality or favoritism (James 2:9) and an unbiblical hatred for humanity (1 John 4:20). The story of creation tells us that Adam and Eve were created in God's image. We can use the creation story to teach our children that every person is made in the image of God, who has no favorites. God sent his only Son to die for all his people, everywhere, because all people, everywhere, are sinful and in need of salvation. The playing field is level at the foot of the cross, so no one can look down on anyone—we're all sinners in need of grace.

Let's look more closely at how James, Jesus's half-brother, addresses the sin of favoritism. He says, "My brothers, do not show favoritism as you hold on to the faith in our glorious Lord Jesus Christ" (James 2:1). James is clear in this verse that favoritism dishonors God and demeans mercy. What is favoritism? Favoritism is a word that means "to turn face" or "to lift up someone's face"; it carries the idea of judging based on appearance.[1]

Paul echoes James's sentiments in Romans:

> He will repay each one according to his works: eternal life to those who by persistence in doing good seek glory, honor, and immortality; but wrath and anger to those who are self-seeking and disobey the truth while obeying unrighteousness. There will be affliction and distress for every human being who does evil, first to the Jew, and also to the Greek; but glory, honor, and peace for everyone who does what is good, first to the Jew, and also to the Greek. For there is no favoritism with God. (Romans 2:6–11)

Notice how James connects holding on to the faith by not showing favoritism, but instead by seeking to glorify the Lord Jesus Christ, and Paul does the same in Romans. We do this by seeing the image of God in *all* people. When we devalue people by judging them externally, we're acting like we're not recipients of mercy ourselves, thus missing the entire point of redemption. We're blessed when we realize our spiritual poverty (Matthew 5:3) and need of salvation. If we realize our spiritual poverty, then it should be impossible to look down on anyone based on what we see externally.

Even a quick overview of what the Bible says about the sin of favoritism makes it clear that the sin of racism fits in this category. My working definition of racism is willful hatred of an entire group of people based on race; it's the sin of partiality applied to someone's race and ethnic background (James 2:1–13). It is important to name racism as sin. Just as we acknowledge that murder, stealing, cheating, and adultery are sins that start in the heart and emerge in words and actions, so we should acknowledge that this is also true of racism.

Most Christians would acknowledge that racism is wrong, and that is certainly a good start when talking with your children. It is also vital to think of it on a spectrum, to avoid loosely labeling everyone a racist when there could be other factors that are applicable. This also empowers you as a parent to avoid teaching your children to think of race in binary ways that could be unhelpful or even harmful. Many people are simply ignorant about people of a different race—they are not around folks of other ethnic backgrounds. Others are indifferent and even uncaring about the problems and struggles of other ethnic groups. Still others are insensitive to issues of racism. While ignorance, indifference, and insensitivity are not the same as willful hatred, they still must be challenged. As parents, we must prepare our children with a biblical anthropology and appreciation of the differences God has created us all with. While it may not be the subject every Sunday in the church or every discussion over dinner after school, it shouldn't be avoided either.

How do we combat racial ignorance, indifference, insensitivity, and racism? Christians are supposed to be unstained by the world, and that means we don't assign value to people the way the world does. The world we live in evaluates a person's value externally: looks, income, weight, gender, and in many cases, race. Therefore, in order to avoid racial ignorance, indifference, and insensitivity, as well as outright racism, we should ask ourselves: Do I judge based on external appearances? Have my experiences caused me to wrongly judge an entire group of people? Am I comfortable with internal prejudice as long as I don't say it? Do I value people based on their contribution or their Creator? As Christian parents, we should teach our children to actively work against any attitude that ignores or demeans those made in God's image. Here are some ways to begin the hard work of talking with your children about racism.

How to Talk with Your Kids about Race

1. Start with Yourself

Pray, meditate, read Scripture, learn from trusted Christian sources on this topic, read, reflect, and consider your thoughts within community instead of in isolation. Keep talking and asking questions—honest questions to learn and apply what the Scripture says on these matters. Invest as much time as you can in reading books, listening to sermons, going to conferences, sitting in on webinars, and conversing with people who can support you in your learning journey. Additionally, spend an equal amount of time thinking about your conversations and paying attention to your physical and emotional reactions during those conversations.

This isn't to be done legalistically or to think that doing this will magically answer all of your questions. The point is to grow, in order to be able to lovingly invest in your children. It's also important to assess your own relationships. Are you and your family in relationship with folks from different racial and ethnic backgrounds? If not, what can you do to widen your community? The early church brought people together from all different backgrounds. Even a quick read of Acts shows us that this wasn't easy and that there were tensions between different people groups, but the early church worked hard on these issues (see, for example, Acts 6:1–7).

2. Have Open and Honest Conversation

Children quickly learn that not everyone will agree with them or share their worldview, especially on the topic of race, so it's important that you, as the parent, have honest conversations with them. One way to equip yourself is by having conversations about these issues outside of homogenous settings. I'm grateful for my brothers and sisters who don't look like me but are willing to listen and change. I'm willing to extend the same respect because all sides have blind spots, and your children need to see you model this.

This doesn't mean that your posture should be to "sit down and shut up"; rather, your goal is to disagree without being disrespectful. While these conversations are hard and at times frustrating, a posture that says "sit down and shut up" is the antithesis of what Paul calls "speaking the truth in love" (Ephesians 4:15–16). Because, as Paul points out, we must all grow together In Christ, we (followers of Christ) must refuse to give into "cancel culture" and writing people off—because recipients of grace have no right to permanently cancel anyone. Christ has cancelled our eternal debt, and that cancellation must keep us from cancelling and dismissing others (Colossians 2:14). Don't be afraid to talk with others about racism, police brutality, systemic injustice, etc. Just be sure to root your dialogue in Scripture. Racism is the sin of partiality or favoritism (James 2:9) and hatred for humanity (1 John 4:20) and is completely inconsistent with God's call for us to love even our enemies (Matthew 5:43–48). Teach your children that sin has caused some to judge people based on skin color, and that this sin began when all sin did—when Adam and Eve went their own way instead of God's way. However, remind them that Jesus has given value to every person (Genesis 1:26; Galatians 3:28).

Being honest about issues will not totally prepare your children for every experience they may encounter, but taking an active role to teach them about race will certainly keep them from being blindsided. Why? *Reconciliation is impossible without confrontation.* Even Christ had to confront the issue of sin in order for us to be reconciled to God. Christ has empowered you to confront these issues, to have these conversations, and to equip your child with a gospel-centered view of race.

3. Teach Them That Differences Don't Have to Be Divisive

Dr. Jarvis Williams says the category of race has a broader use in the Bible than in modern terminology. One important distinction is that the biblical category of race was not something constructed with pseudoscience for the purpose of establishing a racial hierarchy. Racial categories were employed apart from any consideration of biological inferiority rooted in whiteness or blackness. In fact, Genesis 11:6 identifies humanity as one *genos* (race/kind/class/group). The Greek term *ethnos* (nation, Gentile) overlaps with *genos*. Both terms function as racial categories.[2] This means that while we may look different, we have more in common than we think. Knowing this helps you to emphasize biblical unity and teach your children how to do the same. Whether you see race as a social construct or not, the reality is that the differences are evident but don't have to be divisive, so teach your children to move in a spirit of love.

Teach your children what pastor D. A. Horton calls *ethnic conciliation*. Horton says, "Ethnic conciliation is accomplished when we affirm (not ignore or idolize) the ethnic heritage of every human being and seek to remove animosity, distrust, and hostility from our interpersonal relationships."[3] If conciliation is realized, then thoughts, trends, and methods that oppose it are both confronted and resisted, and unity can be championed. Teaching this to your children empowers them to appreciate the physical differences God has given humanity, not as barometers of value but as marks of God's creative genius. They will meet classmates with interracial parents, classmates with parents of the same race, and classmates who are the recipients of transracial adoptions. When you're intentional about teaching them to appreciate differences, you're equipping your child to be a tangible display of the gospel. Teach them that's it's not the color of their skin that matters, but rather the condition of their soul, and unleash them to be willing to share the gospel with anyone!

4. Teach Them to Be Color-Engaging, Not Colorblind

The gospel isn't colorblind; it's color-engaging. Many parents assume the answer to racial disparities or differences is to teach their children to be colorblind, but it isn't. The gospel doesn't deny differences or demand that we should be blind to them. The gospel-rich, color-engaging message of hope we have doesn't need to be blind to color, but rather should be one that celebrates differences and displays the courage to confront issues that threaten unity and demean entire people groups. Sadly, colorblindness often becomes truth-blindness. As Thatbiti Anyabwile says,

> The color-blind approach proceeds on a misdiagnosis of the problem. Seeing color in the physical sense of seeing is *not* the problem. Unless one is actually blind, we all see color. Admitting that people have skin pigments of varying hues and that sometimes those hues cluster into what the

Bible calls families, clans, kinsmen, and nations is *not* the problem. Again, that's self-evident. Anyone denying these things (and I'm not aware of any who does) is simply being delusional or dishonest.[4]

God created color and ethnicity by creating all people in his image (Genesis 1:26). A kingdom ethic is one that sees the differences within humanity as one aspect of the mosaic known as humanity, created by a God who can create something from nothing. My hope is that "colorblindness" will be rejected and "color-engaging" accepted as a true kingdom approach to humanity. After all, John sees every tribe, tongue, and nation in the book of Revelation (Revelation 7:9).

Scripture isn't colorblind, and followers of Christ shouldn't be either. While teaching our children not to be colorblind, we should always be intentional in letting them know that we must never make a feature of who we are the foundation of our identity. Our identity is in Christ, which means *he* gives our lives meaning, purpose, and value (Philippians 3:7–11). When you teach your children that Christ is the foundation of their identity, they're free to appreciate and have an affinity for their culture, but not in an exclusionary or prejudicial way. Teach them that they don't need to be blind to their own color or the color of others, but to never place color above Christ.

5. Teach Them That God Creates a People from All People

As mentioned earlier, Paul, in talking to the Athenians, says, "From one man He has made every nationality to live over the whole earth and has determined their appointed times and the boundaries of where they live" (Acts 17:26). In essence, we all have the same origin. This means that the very notion of racial superiority is foolish, not to mention completely unbiblical. Teach your children that we all come from the same gene pool, and that we are one in Christ.

As a parent you must wrestle with the reality of racism. Talks about race are essential for equipping your child as kingdom citizens in a world that will both disagree with and dismiss them. Since racism is a spiritual problem (James 2:9) that traces all the way back to the garden of Eden (Genesis 3), the answer is spiritual renewal, which has been and will always be provided by Christ. Teaching your children the spiritually renewing, injustice-confronting, liberating, unifying, and saving gospel is critical to your role as a parent. Christ has torn down the dividing walls:

> But now in Christ Jesus you who once were far off have been brought near by the blood of Christ. For he himself is our peace, who has made us both one and has broken down

in his flesh the dividing wall of hostility. (Ephesians 2:13–14 ESV)

Dividers, like the ones used in offices, are designed to section off space. We have heart dividers to section off parts of our hearts from people. But Christ, who is our (and by "our" we mean all believers—Jew, Gentile, black, white, Hispanic, Indian, Latino, Asian and on and on) peace has torn down the wall of separation. In Christ, we're "a people" unified around his finished work.

6. Rely on the Spirit for Difficult Discussions

I know it's not easy to have these discussions. When my son saw the shootings of unarmed black men at the hands of police, he was confused and had questions while his sister was crying in the other room. This wasn't easy for my wife and me. I didn't jettison all cops or make assumptions about the outcome. I allowed them to process their emotions, pointed them to the Scriptures, prayed, and highlighted how everyone has value and explained why we need Jesus. This wasn't their first experience like this and it won't be their last, but we're giving them a biblical blueprint for handling heartbreaking situations, and you can too. It's not easy to talk about race with your kids, but it's a challenge you and I must take up, speaking the truth in love and relying on the Spirit to equip us with what to say, when to listen and when to repent when we blow it. Simply put, we must trust the Spirit of God in the process. As Jarvis Williams says, "Together we're called to celebrate the beauty of the gospel in color, to proclaim our unity within our diversity—and to teach our kids to do the same."[5]

Final Thoughts on Why We Should Have These Difficult Discussions

It's important to initiate gospel-saturated conversations with our kids about race, because a Christian response to this difficult topic helps them understand how to do good works in light of Jesus's finished work! Paul, in his letter to Titus, says, "For the grace of God has appeared, bringing salvation for all people, instructing us to deny godlessness and worldly lusts and to live in a sensible, righteous, and godly way in the present age, while we wait for the blessed hope, the appearing of the glory of our great God and Savior, Jesus Christ. He gave Himself for us to redeem us from all lawlessness and to cleanse for Himself a people for His own possession, eager to do good works" (Titus 2:11–14). We aren't motivated by guilt; instead we are motivated by the desire to do the good work of justice based on God delivering justice to all humanity. Talking to your children about race and injustice isn't political or socially driven; it's a biblical mandate.

We should pursue justice because it is on God's heart. Isaiah says, "Wash yourselves. Cleanse yourselves. Remove your evil deeds from my sight. Stop doing evil. Learn to do what is good. Pursue justice. Correct the oppressor. Defend the rights of the fatherless. Plead the widow's cause" (Isaiah 1:16–17). We don't withhold justice for personal comfort or out of fear of being shunned by those who may wrongly label us because of our fight for justice, equality, and unity. Jesus continues this theme by saying, "Woe to you, scribes and Pharisees, hypocrites! You pay a tenth of mint, dill, and cumin, and yet you have neglected the more important matters of the law— justice, mercy, and faithfulness. These things should have been done without neglecting the others. Blind guides! You strain out a gnat, but gulp down a camel!" (Matthew 23:23–24).

We don't shy away from the topic of injustice because we also remember the injustice we have done against God! In Micah 6, the people asked four questions: "With what shall I come before the LORD, and bow myself before God on high? Shall I come before him with burnt offerings, with calves a year old? Will the Lord be pleased with thousands of rams, with ten thousands of rivers of oil?" (vv. 6–7a ESV). The fourth question was, "Shall I give my firstborn for my transgression, the fruit of my body for the sin of my soul?" (v. 7b ESV). We don't have to sacrifice our firstborn—because God gave up his! Since God gave his Son for us, we can honor his sacrifice and fulfill the law of love by giving up our preferences that exclude others. Because we know that we have peace with God because of Jesus's death and resurrection, we can have the courage to confront our fears.

The gospel is what drives us as parents to have the difficult but necessary conversations surrounding race and justice. This is certainly one of the good works that God has prepared in advance for us as parents to do. Let's step into these conversations by faith, remembering that the same Jesus who died for all his people will certainly be with us as we tackle this difficult subject and model God's love to our children.

Endnotes

1. "Partiality," SermonIndex.net, https://www.sermonindex.net/modules/articles/index.php?view=article&aid=34571 (accessed March 2021).

2. Jarvis J. Williams and Kevin M. Jones, *Removing the Stain of Racism from the Southern Baptist Convention: Diverse African American and White Perspectives* (Nashville: B&H Academic, 2017), 27.

3. D. A. Horton, *Intensional: Kingdom Ethnicity in a Divided Word* (Colorado Springs: NavPress, 2019), 12.

4. Thabiti Anyabwile, "When Color Blind Is Truth Blind," The Gospel Coalition, May 15, 2018, https://www.thegospelcoalition.org/blogs/thabitianyabwile/color-blind-truth-blind.

5. Custis A. Woods and Jarvis J. Williams, "Why to Teach the Gospel and Not Racial Reconciliation," The Witness, May 18, 2018, https://thewitnessbcc.com/why-teach-your-kids-about-the-gospel-and-racial-reconciliation.